Informing the legislative debate since 1914 _____

Millennium Challenge Corporation

Curt Tarnoff
Specialist in Foreign Affairs

July 1, 2014

Congressional Research Service

7-5700

www.crs.gov

RL32427

Summary

The Millennium Challenge Corporation (MCC) provides economic assistance through a competitive selection process to developing nations that demonstrate positive performance in three areas: ruling justly, investing in people, and fostering economic freedom.

Established in 2004, the MCC differs in several respects from past and current U.S. aid practices:

- the competitive process that rewards countries for past actions measured by objective performance indicators;

- its mandate to seek poverty reduction through economic growth, not encumbered with multiple sector objectives;

- the requirement to solicit program proposals developed solely by qualifying countries with broad-based civil society involvement;

- the responsibility of recipient countries to implement their own MCC-funded programs, known as compacts;

- a compact duration limited to five years, with funding committed up front;

- the expectation that compact projects will have measurable impact; and

- an emphasis on public transparency in every aspect of agency operations.

On January 17, 2014, the President signed P.L. 113-76, the Consolidated Appropriations Act, 2014, providing the MCC with $898.2 million in FY2014, matching the Administration request.

On March 4, 2014, the Administration issued its FY2015 State, Foreign Operations budget request. It would provide $1 billion for the MCC, an 11% increase over the FY2014 appropriation. On June 27, 2014, the House Appropriations Committee reported H.R. 5013, the FY2015 State, Foreign Operations appropriations, providing $898.2 million for the MCC, $101.8 million less than the Administration request and the same amount appropriated in FY2014. On June 19, 2014, the Senate Appropriations Committee reported S. 2499, the FY2015 State, Foreign Operations appropriations, providing $901 million for the MCC, $99 million less than the Administration request and $2.8 million more than the amount appropriated in FY2014.

Congress authorized the MCC in P.L. 108-199 (January 23, 2004). Since that time, the MCC's Board of Directors has approved 28 grant agreements, known as compacts: with Madagascar (calendar year 2005), Honduras (2005), Cape Verde (2005), Nicaragua (2005), Georgia (2005), Benin (2006), Vanuatu (2006), Armenia (2006), Ghana (2006), Mali (2006), El Salvador (2006), Mozambique (2007), Lesotho (2007), Morocco (2007), Mongolia (2007), Tanzania (2007), Burkina Faso (2008), Namibia (2008), Senegal (2009), Moldova (2009), Philippines (2010), Jordan (2010), Malawi (2011), Indonesia (2011), Cape Verde II (2011), Zambia (2012), Georgia II (2013), and El Salvador II (2013, not yet signed).

MCC issues include the level of funding to support MCC programs, the results of MCC compacts, sustainability and corruption concerns.

Contents

Tables

Appendixes

Contacts

Most Recent Developments

On June 27, 2014, the House Appropriations Committee reported H.R. 5013, the FY2015 State, Foreign Operations appropriations, providing $898.2 million for the MCC, $101.8 million less than the Administration request and the same amount appropriated in FY2014.

On June 19, 2014, the Senate Appropriations Committee reported S. 2499, the FY2015 State, Foreign Operations appropriations, providing $901 million for the MCC, $99 million less than the Administration request and $2.8 million more than the amount appropriated in FY2014.

On May 20, 2014, the Senate confirmed the nomination of Dana J. Hyde to be CEO of the MCC.

On March 4, 2014, the Administration issued its FY2015 State, Foreign Operations budget request. It would provide $1 billion for the MCC, an 11% increase over the FY2014 appropriation.

On January 17, 2014, the President signed P.L. 113-76, the Consolidated Appropriations Act, 2014, providing the MCC with $898.2 million in FY2014, matching the Administration request and a 5% increase over the FY2013 post-sequester level. The legislation would also prohibit a threshold program going to any country not currently eligible for candidacy, effectively excluding FY2011-eligible Tunisia, which is now an upper-middle income country.

On December 10, 2013, the MCC Board selected Lesotho as eligible for a second compact, and reselected Liberia and Niger for first compacts and Ghana, Morocco, and Tanzania for second compacts. Although Liberia and Morocco were reselected despite passing less than half the qualifying indicators, the Board indicated final compact approval depended on their eventually meeting the scorecard requirements. The Board did not reselect Benin and Sierra Leone, approved in FY2013, because they did not pass the control of corruption scorecard indicator. The Board also reselected Guatemala and Nepal for threshold program eligibility.

In September 2013, President Obama nominated Dana J. Hyde to become the CEO of the MCC. Current CEO Daniel Yohannes is stepping down. On November 19, a nomination hearing was held in the Senate Foreign Relations Committee and the nomination was favorably reported on December 18. The nomination has not yet been confirmed by the Senate.

On September 12, 2013, the MCC Board approved a $277 million compact with El Salvador. The second compact addresses the investment climate, human capital and the labor market, and infrastructure benefitting the economy. The compact has not yet been signed.

Introduction

The Millennium Challenge Corporation (MCC), established in 2004, arose out of a widespread frustration with then-existing foreign aid programs and represented a significant change in the way the United States delivered economic assistance. The MCC is based on the premise that economic development succeeds best where it is linked to free market economic and democratic principles and policies, and where governments are committed to implementing reform measures in order to achieve such goals. The MCC concept differs in several fundamental respects from past and current U.S. aid practices:

- a competitive process that rewards countries for their commitment to free market economic and democratic policies as measured by objective performance indicators;

- the pledge to segregate the funds from U.S. strategic foreign policy objectives that often strongly influence where U.S. aid is spent;

- its mandate to seek poverty reduction through economic growth, not encumbered with multiple sector objectives or earmarks;

- the requirement to solicit program proposals developed solely by qualifying countries with broad-based civil society involvement;

- the responsibility of recipient countries to implement their own MCC-funded programs, known as compacts;

- a compact duration limited to five years, with funding committed up front;

- the expectation that compact projects will have measurable impact; and

- an emphasis on public transparency in every aspect of agency operations.

The original proposal, made by President George W. Bush in a speech on March 14, 2002, also differed from previous aid efforts in the size of its commitment to reach an annual level of $5 billion within a few years, an aim never even approximately met.

Congress approved the new initiative in January 2004 in the Millennium Challenge Act of 2003 (Division D of P.L. 108-199).[1] It established the MCC as an independent government entity separate from the Departments of State and the Treasury and from the U.S. Agency for International Development (USAID).[2] The MCC headquarters staff level is currently about 268, with a total of 25 additional U.S. direct hire employees in compact countries.[3] In May 2014, Dana J. Hyde became the new Chief Executive Officer (CEO) of the MCC. A Board of Directors oversees the MCC and makes the country selections. It is chaired by the Secretary of State and composed of the Secretary of the Treasury, the USAID Administrator, the U.S. Trade

---

[1] When first proposed and in its early years, the initiative was known as the Millennium Challenge Account. Today, both the program and the funding account in the foreign operations budget are more commonly known by the name of the managing entity, the MCC. For a more in-depth discussion of the original MCC proposal and issues debated by Congress in 2003, see CRS Report RL31687, *The Millennium Challenge Account: Congressional Consideration of a New Foreign Aid Initiative*, by Larry Nowels.

[2] The decision to house the initiative in a new organization was one of the most debated issues during early congressional deliberations. The Bush Administration argued that because the initiative represents a new concept in aid delivery, it should have a "fresh" organizational structure, unencumbered by bureaucratic authorities and regulations that would interfere in effective management. Critics, however, contended that if the initiative was placed outside the formal U.S. government foreign aid structure, it would lead to further fragmentation of policy development and consistency. Some believed that USAID, the principal U.S. aid agency, should manage the program, while others said that it should reside in the State Department. At least, some argued, the USAID Administrator should be a member of the MCC Board, which had not been proposed in the initial Administration request.

[3] MCC, *Agency Financial Report, Fiscal Year 2013*, p. 12.

Representative, the Corporation's CEO, and four individuals from the private sector appointed by the President drawn from lists submitted by congressional leaders.[4]

Since its inception, Congress has closely followed MCC implementation. The 113th Congress will likely consider MCC funding, a possible reauthorization, and operational issues.

MCC Policy and Programs

Since the MCC was launched, procedures and policies have continued to evolve. Program implementation moves chronologically through a number of steps: candidate countries are identified, eligibility criteria are formulated and applied, compact and threshold-eligible countries are selected, compact programs are developed and proposed, and those approved are funded and carried out. Elements in this process are discussed below.

Identification of Candidate Countries

The pool of possible candidate countries is limited by the authorizing statute to those falling under the threshold for the World Bank's classification for upper-middle income countries. For FY2014, this limit is a Gross National Income (GNI) per capita of $4,085. As a result, the pool of possible candidates is 83 countries for FY2014.[5]

Apart from the necessity to be under the income ceiling, income level status—in particular, the division of candidate countries between lower-income and lower-middle income—is important in both the financing and competitive selection processes and, since FY2012, has been treated differently in each case. See "Selection of Compact-Eligible Countries" below for competitive selection discussion.

Until FY2012, the pool of possible participants for funding purposes, as defined by Section 606 of the MCC authorization, included low-income countries—those with a Gross National Income (GNI) per capita below the World Bank's International Development Association (IDA) eligibility level of $1,965 (in FY2014)—and lower-middle income countries—defined as those between that figure and $4,085 (in FY2014), the threshold for the Bank's classification for upper-middle income countries.[6]

---

[4] Current private sector board members serving their first term are Susan M. McCue, president of Message Global, and Morton Halperin, senior advisor for the Open Society Foundations. Serving a second term is Lorne Craner, co-director of the Transatlantic Renewal Initiative, and Mark Green, president of the International Republican Institute. First terms run three years and second terms run two years.

[5] A change to upper-income status excludes a country from consideration for new programs, unless the MCC Board had selected that country as eligible in a previous year (when the country qualified as lower-middle income or below) and is able to fund the program using that previous year's funds. In FY2011, Albania, a threshold program country, moved to upper-middle-income status and, therefore, became ineligible for MCC compact assistance. On the other hand, Namibia, which gained upper-middle-income status in FY2008 and Jordan in FY2012, were able to continue their on-going compacts as they were selected and signed compacts prior to the change in status.

[6] The MCC draws on World Bank income data published in the July preceding the MCC's August report identifying candidates for the following fiscal year. As there is a lag in data collection, the July 2013 report, for example, provides 2012 data that is used in the FY2014 MCC candidacy and compact-eligibility process. Note that the IDA low-income eligibility figure differs from the standard World Bank classification of low income countries.

However, this division of countries into income groups and the high annual volatility of income level data created some uncertainties and problems.[7] Under the MCC legislative authority, only a quarter of total MCC compact assistance in any year is available for lower-middle income country compacts, severely limiting the possibility that such countries can be funded and therefore discouraging the MCC Board from selecting them. Countries moving from one income level to another had no predictable path to compact eligibility. Both the Philippines (FY2009) and Indonesia (FY2009) were first selected when they were low-income countries; a year later they transitioned to lower-middle income and were subject to the lower-middle income funding cap. This abrupt shift was viewed by the MCC as extremely disruptive to a smooth-functioning compact development process. A further concern is the diminishing pool of well-governed candidates eligible for the larger amount of lower-income funding as more countries have been transitioning into the lower-middle level.

To address this recurring issue of income category change, the FY2014 continuing appropriations (P.L. 113-46) carries forward FY2012 appropriations language (P.L. 112-74) that, for purposes of funding eligibility, redefines the category of low-income countries from the previously noted definition of those with per capita incomes below $1,965 (in FY2014) to one that encompasses the bottom 75 countries in the low- and lower-middle income level rankings. The remaining countries below the World Bank's cut-off ceiling for lower-middle income countries ($4,085 per capita in FY2014) remain defined as lower-middle in MCC terms. Applied in FY2014, 74 countries are considered for MCC funding purposes as low-income and 9 countries are considered lower-middle income (versus 56 and 27, respectively, under the old definition).[8]

Seeking to further ensure stability and predictability for candidate countries that might be transitioning in and out of different income levels, the FY2012 appropriations language, carried forward to FY2014, requires that countries that move from low-income to lower-middle income or vice versa be treated as though they are in their former classification for that fiscal year and two succeeding years.[9] MCC believes this legislation provides for a graduated transition for countries rather than the abrupt change in status that characterized the previous process.

In addition to the income ceiling, under the MCC authorization, countries may be candidates only if they are not statutorily prohibited from receiving U.S. economic assistance. For FY2014, 15 countries were excluded for this reason. Many had been barred in prior years as well.[10] Two,

---

[7] An example of the limitations of determining eligibility based on variable factors like income level is the Philippines. The Philippines was selected for compact eligibility as a low-income country in FY2008 (and signed a compact based on that status in 2010), moved from low-income to the lower-middle-income level in FY2010, then returned to low-income status in FY2011, and again to lower-middle-income status in FY2012 where it has remained since.

[8] 74 in FY2014, instead of 75, because Iraq leapt from low income to upper-middle income, and application of the legislative provision that holds countries at their income status for three years, leaves a gap of one from the base year of FY2012.

[9] In an early version of this provision, the FY2010 Consolidated Appropriations Act (P.L. 111-117, H.R. 3288, Division F) allowed those transitioning countries already selected in FY2009 to maintain their candidacy for eligibility and, if re-selected, draw on the same source of funds as when they were first selected. The compact for Indonesia, transitioning to lower-middle in FY2010 when it was re-selected, was therefore funded as though in the low-income group.

[10] Various types of aid restrictions applied to these countries. For Sudan, Madagascar, Mali, and Guinea-Bissau, U.S. aid was blocked because an elected head of government had been deposed by a military coup. For Zimbabwe, legislation banned assistance to the central government until rule of law is restored. For Cameroon, Central African Republic, the Gambia, Madagascar, Nicaragua, and Swaziland, aid is prohibited to the central government of countries not meeting minimum standards of fiscal transparency. Aid restrictions imposed on nations that support international terrorism (Sudan, Syria, North Korea), or in arrears on debt owed the United States (Syria, Sudan) also applied. (continued...)

Madagascar and Mali, excluded in FY2010 and FY2012, respectively, because of an undemocratic change in government, were compact countries at the time, and had their MCC compact programs terminated early.

In August 2013, the MCC transmitted to Congress its annual notification of candidate countries.[11] For funding purposes, the revised version listed 59 low-income countries (from the original pool of 74, after excluding prohibited countries) and 9 lower-middle-income countries.

Compact-Eligible Country Selection Criteria and Methodology

As noted earlier, the MCC provides assistance to developing nations through a competitive selection process, judged by country performance in three areas:

- Ruling justly—promoting good governance, fighting corruption, respecting human rights, and adhering to the rule of law.

- Investing in people—providing adequate health care, education, and other opportunities promoting an educated and healthy population.

- Economic freedom—fostering enterprise and entrepreneurship and promoting open markets and sustainable budgets.

Country selection is based largely, *but not exclusively*, on a nation's record, measured by performance indicators related to these three categories, or "baskets." Indicators may be a straightforward single measure of a country's rate of inflation—one reflection of good economic policies—or may be a combination of data points forming an index of surveys and expert opinions on the quality of public service, civil servant competency, a government's ability to plan and implement sound policies, which together "measure" government effectiveness. MCC is constrained somewhat in measuring performance by the public availability of appropriate, comparable, and consistent data on every country.

The choice of criteria on which to base the eligibility of countries for MCC programs is one of the most important elements in MCC operations. They are a key statement of MCC development priorities as they ultimately determine which countries will receive U.S. assistance. Perhaps of equal significance, raising indicator scores has become a prominent objective of some developing countries in what former CEO Danilovich called the "MCC effect."[12] Countries seeking eligibility are said to be moving on their own to enact reforms and take measures to improve performance scores that would enable them to meet MCC criteria.

Pursuant to reporting requirements set in the MCC legislation, each year the Corporation sends to Congress an overview of the criteria and methodology that would be used to determine the eligibility of the candidate countries in that fiscal year.[13] The criteria have been altered and

---

(...continued)

Notwithstanding these and other restrictions, each country remained eligible for humanitarian assistance from the United States.

[11] MCC, *Report on Countries that are Candidates for Millennium Challenge Account Eligibility for Fiscal Year 2014 and Countries that would be Candidates but for Legal Prohibitions*, August 2013.

[12] MCC Public Outreach Meeting, February 15, 2007.

[13] Most recently, *Report on the Criteria and Methodology for Determining the Eligibility of Candidate Countries for* (continued...)

refined, sometimes dramatically, over time. In September 2011, the MCC Board adopted for the FY2012 process perhaps the most significant changes to its selection methods since the agency was established. These continue to be applied in FY2014.

For most performance indicators, each country is judged against its peers in its income group, requiring a score just above the median to pass that indicator. For some indicators there is an absolute threshold that must be met in order to pass the indicator. The absolute threshold indicators include an "inflation rate" under 15%, "political rights" requiring a score above 17, "civil liberties" requiring a score above 25, and, for lower-middle-income countries only, an "immunization coverage" of above 90%.

Countries are required to pass at least half of the total number of indicators—10 of the 20 indicators (see **Appendix D** for a complete list of the 20 performance indicators). Of the 10, two of these are "hard hurdles" that must be passed to qualify—the "control of corruption" indicator and either one of two democratic rights indicators, the "civil liberties" indicator or the "political rights" indicator. Requiring passage of a democratic rights indicator may weed out countries that achieved eligibility only to have their compact programs suspended or terminated when their governments failed to meet governance performance standards. Finally, to avoid concerns that a country could achieve compact eligibility with a passing performance in only two of the three baskets, the Board set the requirement that countries must pass at least one indicator in each basket.

Periodically, the MCC establishes some indicators and modifies or replaces old ones in an effort to improve the quality of indicators and identify indicators better reflecting congressional intent. Beginning with the FY2005 selection process, for example, the MCC lowered the inflation rate threshold from 20% to 15%, making it somewhat more difficult to pass this test (only 6 of the 63 candidate countries failed this test for FY2004). For FY2006, the MCC replaced a "country credit rating" with a new indicator on the "cost of starting a business" that it believed had a stronger correlation with economic growth and was a measurement that might encourage governments to take action in order to improve their scores. Since the initial use of the indicator "days to start a business," MCC candidate countries had introduced many business start-up reforms, the results of which were reflected in a lowered median for this category. MCC officials hoped that adding an indicator for the "cost of starting a business" would stimulate additional policy improvements. In FY2008, the MCC collapsed the "days to start a business" and "cost of starting a business" indicators into one "business start-up" indicator.

In addition to criteria originally proposed by the Bush Administration, lawmakers in the 2004 MCC authorizing legislation included four other matters on which to evaluate a country's performance. These relate to the degree to which a country recognizes the rights of people with disabilities; respects worker rights; supports a sustainable management of natural resources; and makes social investments, especially in women and girls. For each of these, the MCC has sought to use supplemental data and qualitative information to inform its decisions on compact eligibility. The latter two factors have led to the development of new indicators. In FY2005, an indicator measuring girls' primary education completion rates replaced a broader measure used in FY2004 that did not disaggregate primary education graduation by gender. In FY2008, two

---

(...continued)

Millennium Challenge Account Assistance in Fiscal Year 2014, September 2013.

indicators assessing a country's commitment to policies that promote sustainable management of natural resources were adopted.

In FY2012, the MCC modified or added new indicators under all three baskets. Under the Ruling Justly basket, a "freedom of information" indicator, including a measure of efforts to restrict internet content, replaced the "voice and accountability" indicator. Under Investing in People, a measure of "natural resource management" was split into two indicators, one focusing on "natural resource protection" that assesses whether countries are protecting up to 10% of their biomes, and the other on "child health," which captures the earlier indicator's data on access to improved water, sanitation, and child mortality. The indicator on girls' education was amended solely for lower-middle-income countries to weigh the number of female students enrolled in secondary school, rather than those completing primary school, which remains the indicator for low-income countries.

Two new indicators were added to the Economic Freedom category of performance measures. An "access to credit" indicator reflects the importance of credit in stimulating private sector growth. A "gender in the economy" indicator measures a government's commitment to promote equal economic legal rights for both men and women.

Selection of Compact-Eligible Countries

Shortly after release of the performance criteria, the MCC publishes a scorecard, showing where each candidate country's performance falls in relation to the other candidate countries in its peer group and where they stand on the absolute threshold indicators. Some time later, the MCC Board meets to select countries eligible to apply for compact assistance.

It is MCC practice that low-income countries "compete" with other low-income countries and lower-middle income countries with other lower-middle income countries. With regard to the competitive selection process that determines compact eligibility, the original income level definitions in the MCC authorization still apply, not those established in FY2012 for funding purposes.[14] In the FY2014 selection process, there are 44 low-income countries competing with each other, and 24 lower-middle income countries competing with each other, a total of 68 candidate countries from which compact-eligible countries may be chosen. (See **Appendix C**.)

The Board is guided by, but not entirely bound to, the outcome of the performance indicator review process; board members can apply discretion in their selection. Performance trends, missing or old data, and recent policy actions might come into play during selection deliberations. For countries being considered for second compacts, the history and success of implementation of the first compact is a significant factor.

Because it is MCC practice to judge the performance of countries within their income status cohort, countries that move from one year to the next from low-income to lower-middle income status may be affected negatively by being compared to countries longer established at a higher level of development. Seeking to mitigate the negative consequences of income change, in September 2009, the MCC Board announced that henceforth, for countries that move from low to

---

[14] For scorecard performance assessments, low-income is defined as below the World Bank's IDA eligibility ceiling and lower-middle income is defined as between the IDA ceiling and below the Bank threshold for upper-middle-income countries. The MCC's 75 country low-income definition is for funding availability purposes only.

lower-middle income status, it would consider their performance relative to both their old income group and the newer one for a period of three years. But it only does this as supplemental information and, to date, has only considered the previous status of those countries it is considering for reselection.

Just because a country passes the requisite number of qualifying indicators does not mean that it will be selected for compact eligibility. This can be due to a variety of reasons, not least of which is the limited funding available to support compacts. The Board is not required to give a reason for its selections and only occasionally offers one. Most often it appears that a country has passed the requisite number of qualifying indicators but is not selected because it scores very poorly— perhaps in the lowest 25th percentile—in one or more of the remaining indicators. For example, in FY2005, the Philippines passed 13 of the then-16 indicators, but was not made eligible, because it scored "substantially below" the median on tests for health expenditures and fiscal policy, and more recent trends indicated the fiscal policy situation was deteriorating further.[15] In FY2006, Bhutan, China, and Vietnam passed enough hurdles but were not chosen based on very low scores on political rights and civil liberties; Uganda passed 12 of the 16 indicators and did not fall significantly below the median on the other four, but was not selected for unexplained reasons.

At times, countries have been deemed compact eligible without meeting a sufficient number of qualifying factors or with weak scores in some qualifying areas. In most such cases, the Board takes into consideration recent policy changes or positive trend lines. For example, in FY2004, the program's first year, several countries (Georgia, Mozambique, and Bolivia) were selected despite having failed the so-called "pass-fail" corruption indicator. Mozambique, which failed on corruption and each of the four "investing in people" indicators, was chosen based on supplemental data that were more current than information available from the primary data sources. This evidence, the Board felt, demonstrated Mozambique's commitment to fighting corruption and improving its performance on health and education. In FY2004, Cape Verde scored poorly on the "trade policy" indicator, but the Board took into account the country's progress towards joining the World Trade Organization and implementing a value added tax to reduce reliance on import tariffs. Lesotho did not score well on the measurement for "days to start a business." The MCC Board, however, took note of Lesotho's creation of a central office to facilitate new business formation and saw positive performance on other factors related to business start-ups. In FY2011, Georgia was invited to submit a proposal for a second compact despite failure in the "investing in people" basket; supplemental information attributing an insufficient score in immunization rates to a temporary shortage of one vaccine helped the Board toward a positive decision.

Even prior to its selection in FY2007, the possible choice of Jordan had come in for severe criticism from some quarters. Freedom House, the organization whose annual Index of Freedom is drawn upon for two of the "ruling justly" indicators, had urged the MCC Board to bypass countries that had low scores on political rights and civil liberties. It argued that countries like Jordan that fell below 4 out of a possible 7 on its index should be automatically disqualified. Jordan, however, did well on three of the other indicators in this category. Several development analysts further argued that Jordan should not be selected, because it is one of the largest

---

[15] Comments by Paul Applegarth, then MCC CEO, at a State Department Foreign Press Center Briefing, November 9, 2004.

recipients of U.S. aid, has access to private sector capital, and is not a democracy.[16] In selecting Jordan, the MCC Board appears not to have been swayed by these arguments.

The Board has, at times, selected a country and then, in future years, and prior to approval of a compact, de-selected it if its qualifying scores worsened or other factors interceded. Although the Gambia was selected in FY2006, its eligibility for MCC assistance was suspended by the MCC Board in June 2006 because of "a disturbing pattern of deteriorating conditions" in half of the 16 qualifying factors. Among the problems cited in this case were human rights abuses, restrictions on civil liberties and press freedom, and worsened anti-corruption efforts.[17] For the 2008 selection process, the MCC Board eliminated Sri Lanka because of the resurgent civil strife that would make a compact problematic. In the FY2009 selection round, the Board decided not to reselect several countries that had been eligible in previous years—Bolivia, Timor-Leste, and Ukraine. In FY2008 and FY2009, both Ukraine and Timor-Leste failed the corruption indicator. Timor-Leste, in addition, failed the "investing in people" basket in those years. Bolivia, however, had passed its indicator test in every year. A hold put on MCC consideration of Bolivia's compact proposal in FY2008 and its exclusion from eligibility in FY2009 appeared likely due to the political tensions existing between it and the United States rather than its performance in development-related matters. In the FY2014 selection round, both Benin and Sierra Leone were not reselected for compact eligibility, because they failed the "control of corruption" indicator.

Some countries have remained eligible despite failing performances in years following their selection. For example, Indonesia, selected in FY2009, failed the corruption indicator, half the indicators, and the investing in people basket in FY2010 and FY2011. It remained compact-eligible and signed a compact in 2011, because Congress allowed it to be judged and funded as a lower income country, in which case it passed the selection requirements. In FY2014, the Board continued the eligibility of Liberia and Morocco, although both failed slightly more than half the 20 indicators (11). While compact development could go forward, the Board indicated that it expected both to pass the scorecard before a compact would be approved.

Except in certain extreme circumstances, described in the "Compact Suspension and Termination" section below, countries that are already implementing compacts are generally unaffected by a decline in performance indicators. Nine of the 19 countries implementing compacts as of January 2011 would not have qualified in FY2011.[18] Georgia and Vanuatu had failed three years in a row; Armenia, El Salvador, Mali, and Mozambique had failed four years in a row. Morocco had failed for five years straight.[19] In FY2012, this picture changed dramatically; of 16 active compacts in November 2011, only 2 would fail under the new system, 5 under the old system. In FY2013, 5 of the 15 active compact countries would fail. In FY2014, 3 of the 10 active compact countries would fail—Indonesia, Moldova, and the Philippines.

In not strictly following the rule of the performance indicators, the MCC has argued that the indicators themselves are imperfect measures of a country's policies and performance. The

---

[16] Freedom House, "Millennium Challenge Corporation Should Hold Countries to Higher Standards of Democratic Governance," November 2, 2006, http://www.freedomhouse.org; Sheila Herrling, Steve Radelet, and Sarah Rose, "Will Politics Encroach in the MCA FY2007 Selection Round? The Cases of Jordan and Indonesia," Center for Global Development, October 30, 2006, http://www.cgdev.org.

[17] MCC Press Release, "The Gambia Suspended From Participation in MCC Compact Program," June 15, 2006.

[18] These are Armenia, Burkina Faso, El Salvador, Georgia, Mali, Mongolia, Morocco, Mozambique, and Vanuatu.

[19] For further discussion, see Casey Dunning, Owen McCarthy, and Sarah Jane Staats, Center for Global Development, *Round Eight of the MCA*, December 3, 2010.

indicators often suffer from lag time, reflecting when the raw data were derived as much as a year or more previously. A country's position vis-à-vis its peers may also fluctuate considerably from year to year without reflecting any significant change in the country's policies. Countries following reasonable policies may fall behind the performance criteria when other countries are improving faster—thereby raising the bar. A shift in position from the low income to lower-middle income group can similarly alter a country's scores as it competes with countries more likely to achieve better indicators than ones in the lower income group. They may also fail when new criteria are introduced which countries have not had an opportunity to address and when institutions measuring performance refine or revise their indicators (as was the case in FY2014).

Country Selection—FY2014

In its FY2014 selection round on December 10, 2013, the MCC Board selected Lesotho for second compact eligibility and reselected countries in the process of preparing their compact proposals—Liberia and Niger for first compacts and Ghana, Morocco, and Tanzania as eligible to develop second compacts. Although Liberia and Morocco were reselected despite passing less than half the qualifying indicators, the Board indicated final compact approval depended on their eventually meeting the scorecard requirements. They took this action, because the main reason for the scorecard failure was a change in the way in which the indicator data was collected and assessed rather than any policy change on the part of the countries. The Board did not reselect Benin and Sierra Leone, approved in FY2013, because they did not pass the control of corruption scorecard indicator. However, because the data showed no sign of policy decline on the part of the two countries, the Board asked MCC to continue "limited engagement" with the two countries, apparently leaving open a door for when the countries pass the indicator. The Board also reselected Guatemala and Nepal for threshold program eligibility. Already-signed compact countries do not need to be reselected each year.

Table 1. Compact-Eligible Countries: FY2014

Low-Income Countries	Lower-Middle-Income Countries
Ghana	
Liberia	Morocco
Lesotho	
Niger	
Tanzania	

MCC Compacts

MCC compacts are grant agreements, none more than five years in length (as required by the MCC authorization), proposed and implemented by countries selected by the MCC Board. Details of each compact and major developments in their implementation are provided in **Appendix B**.

As of late 2013, 31% of MCC compact funding was in the transport sector, mostly roads; 19% was targeted on agriculture; 13% on health, education, and community services; 12% on water supply and sanitation; 6% on energy; 6% on governance; and 2% on financial services. Counting the 27 signed compact countries and one (El Salvador) not-yet-signed, but MCC Board-approved, to date, 53% of compact funding has gone to sub-Saharan African countries, 10% to North Africa and the Middle East, 11% to the former Soviet Union, 12% to Latin America, and 14% to Asia and the Pacific.[20]

Since its inception, the MCC has designed guidelines and procedures for project development and implementation that are followed by all MCC compact countries. These are described below.

Compact Development

Once declared as eligible, countries may prepare and negotiate program proposals with the MCC. The process to develop a compact, from eligibility to signing, is expected to take about 27 months. Only those compact proposals that demonstrate a strong relationship between the proposal and economic growth and poverty reduction will receive funding. With limited funding available and six countries eligible, compact development, like the selection process, is competitive.

While acknowledging that compact proposal contents likely will vary, the MCC expects each to discuss certain matters, including a country's strategy for economic growth and poverty reduction, impediments to the strategy, how MCC aid will overcome the impediments, and the goals expected to be achieved during implementation of the compact; why the proposed program is a high priority for economic development and poverty reduction and why it will succeed; the process through which a public/private dialogue took place in developing the proposal; how the program will be managed and monitored during implementation and sustained after the compact expires; the relationship of other donor activities in the priority area; examples of projects, where appropriate; a multi-year financial plan; and a country's commitment to future progress on MCC performance indicators.

Countries designate an entity, usually composed of government and non-government personnel, to coordinate the formulation of the proposal and act as a point of contact with the MCC. In many cases, a high level of political commitment to the program—country leadership identifying themselves closely with the success of the compact—helps propel compact development forward and continues into implementation.

One of the first steps in the compact development process is the undertaking by the compact-eligible country, possibly in conjunction with MCC economists or consultants, of an analysis of the principal constraints to economic growth and poverty reduction. This report seeks to identify the binding constraints that "are the most severe root causes that deter households and firms from making investments of their financial resources, time, and effort that would significantly increase incomes."[21]

Underscoring the MCC concept of "country-ownership" and the requirement of broad public participation in the development of MCC programs embodied in MCC authorization language, the compact development entity typically launches nationwide discussions regarding the scope and purpose of the MCC grant, with meetings held at the regional and national level that include representation of civil society and the business community. In Namibia, the National Planning Commission charged with developing the compact identified 500 issues as a result of public discussions held throughout the country on the question "What will unlock economic

---

[20] MCC, *Annual MCC Report 2012*, p. 6; and CRS calculations.

[21] MCC, *Compact Development Guidance*, January 2012, p. 15.

development in your region?", narrowing them down to 77, and then just to several.[22] Burkina Faso's consultations reportedly included 3,100 people in all 13 regions.[23]

Public consultation combined with analysis of constraints to growth help focus a country on the range of sectors and possible activities that might go into a compact proposal. Concept papers are developed around many of these ideas. During each step in the development process, the MCC provides feedback to keep the country within MCC parameters.

The eventual results of these public deliberations and concept papers are compact proposals. These proposals often exceed MCC's budget capacity, forcing a process of further prioritization and elimination. Tanzania reportedly suggested a package worth $2 billion; with the elimination of irrigation and education options, they were able to bring it down to $700 million. Namibia's first proposal, at $415 million, was whittled down to $305 million by eliminating irrigated agriculture and roads projects.

Proposals are developed by a country with the guidance of and in consultation with the MCC. To assist in compact development, the MCC may, under Section 609(g) of its authorizing statute, provide so-called pre-compact development grants to assist the country's preparatory activities. Among other things, these grants may be used for design studies, baseline surveys, technical and feasibility studies, environmental and social assessments, ongoing consultations, fees for fiscal and/or procurement agents, and the like. For example, in June 2009, the MCC provided Jordan with a pre-compact development grant of $13.34 million, not counted as part of the final compact. It was used for feasibility studies and other assessments for water and wastewater projects.

One feature of compact proposals is the requirement that sustainability issues be addressed. In the case of road construction, this might mean provisions committing the government to seek to establish transport road funds, a fuel levy, or some other tax to pay for road maintenance in future. For example, as a condition of its compact, Honduras increased its annual road maintenance budget from $37 million to $64 million.[24]

Once a proposal is submitted, the MCC conducts an initial assessment, then, on the basis of that assessment, launches a due diligence review that closely examines all aspects of the proposal, including costs and impacts to see if they are worthy of MCC support. Included in the review is an economic analysis assessing anticipated economic rates of return for the proposed projects and estimating the impact on poverty reduction. At the same time, MCC staff work with the country to refine program elements. Finally, the MCC negotiates a final compact agreement prior to its approval by the MCC Board. The compact is signed but does not enter into force until supplemental agreements on disbursements and procurement are reached.[25]

When the compact enters into force the clock begins to tick on compact implementation and the total amount of funds proposed for the compact are formally obligated (held by the U.S. Treasury until disbursed). Because of the difficulties encountered in trying to undertake a complex set of projects within a set five-year time span, MCC has increasingly sought to front load many planning activities prior to compact signing or entry-into-force, including feasibility studies and

---

[22] Tanzania and Namibia examples in this section are based on author interviews.

[23] Rebecca Schutte, *Burkina Faso Field Report*, Center for Global Development, July 2009.

[24] MCC, *Policy Reforms Matter*, September 9, 2010.

[25] Details on each of the negotiated compacts can be found at the MCC website: http://www.mcc.gov.

project design, which in the case of infrastructure can be a lengthy process. Usually, the first year of operations is consumed by contract design and solicitation for services. In the case of Burkina Faso, however, one analyst noted that the passage of a full year between signing and entry-into-force combined with early action on staff and planning allowed an estimated 60% of procurement to be initiated before entry-into-force.[26]

Compact Implementation

Typically, by the time of compact signing, the entity that was established as point of contact during program development segues into the compact management and oversight body, the "accountable entity" usually known as the MCA. Its board is usually composed of government and non-government officials, including representatives of civil society. The government representatives are usually ministers most closely associated with compact project sectors. The MCA itself may take a variety of forms. In Tanzania, it was a government parastatal established by presidential decree under the Ministry of Finance. In Namibia, it is a separate unit within the ministry-level government National Planning Commission.

Calendar Year	Signed MCC Compacts
2005	Madagascar, Honduras, Cape Verde I, Nicaragua, Georgia I
2006	Benin, Vanuatu, Armenia, Ghana, Mali, El Salvador
2007	Mozambique, Lesotho, Morocco, Mongolia
2008	Tanzania, Burkina Faso, Namibia
2009	Senegal
2010	Moldova, the Philippines, Jordan
2011	Malawi, Indonesia
2012	Cape Verde II, Zambia
2013	Georgia II
2014	

MCA staff will include fiscal and procurement agents, in many cases duties contracted out and in some cases, where the capacity is available, undertaken in-house. In the case of Namibia, for example, procurement started as a contracted function, and, when capacity improved, the contractor was replaced by an MCA-staffed procurement office. The MCA is also responsible for ensuring that accountability requirements concerning audits, monitoring, and evaluation take place. Environmental, gender, and other social requirements embedded in the compact agreement are its responsibility as well. Held to a strict five-year timetable and limited budget, the MCA faces a daunting challenge for most developing countries. For many countries, the process of getting the MCA set up, staffed, and operating was very time consuming and difficult, in some cases causing delays in implementation.

As, perhaps, the most important aspect of compact implementation, MCC procurement processes are a good example of how the MCC is building government capacity at the same time that it provides development project assistance and maintains accountability oversight for the use of U.S. funds. In the course of implementing compacts, the MCA signs hundreds of contracts each year to procure equipment, construct infrastructure, or obtain technical expertise. Under MCC rules, compact procurement processes are based on World Bank procedures, not U.S. federal acquisition requirements or the compact country's own rules. To counter corruption, build capacity, and achieve the maximum value for the cost of goods and services, MCC-approved rules feature transparent, competitive bidding from all firms, regardless of national origin.

---

[26] Rebecca Schutte, Center for Global Development, *Burkina Faso Field Report*, July 2009, p. 1.

According to the MCC, companies from 54 countries have won MCC procurement contracts, U.S. firms winning the most with 15% of the total.[27]

MCC-supported procurements are fixed-price contracts, putting the burden on the contractor to get the work done to meet the agreed price. The MCC has a set of standards and guidelines for all its project contracting. The MCC requires that procurements are preceded by a price reasonableness analysis to ensure that bids are realistic. An independent evaluation panel is selected for each discrete procurement, with all members requiring MCC approval to ensure that appropriate technical expertise is represented. The panel's report is also vetted by the MCC.

Reportedly, several countries have adopted this methodology for their procurements. Cape Verde is applying it to all public procurements. Honduras said it would maintain the program management unit to deal with projects funded by other donors and would apply MCC guidelines for procurement.[28]

The MCC itself has only a very small staff located in-country, composed chiefly of a Resident Country Director and a deputy. To assist in oversight of infrastructure projects, which account for more than half of MCC activities, MCC will often hire an independent engineering consultant. Close cooperation and guidance is also provided by MCC Washington headquarters expert staff at all points of implementation, on procedure as well as on sector technical support. MCC has to sign off on all major steps during implementation, including each disbursement. To reduce the risk of corruption, funding is transferred periodically and directly to contractors following a determination that project performance has continued satisfactorily. An appealing feature of MCC contracts to international contractor firms is that payment is made by the United States Treasury, not the compact country.

Following completion of a compact, the MCC conducts impact or performance evaluations using independent evaluators. Results of the evaluations are being made public. To date, however, only a small fraction of possible evaluations—five farmer training programs—have been released.

As projects are implemented, events may require that changes be made to compact plans.[29] In 2007 and 2008, for example, the convergence of a depreciating U.S. dollar and rising costs for the machines and material necessary for the many infrastructure projects conducted by MCC meant that MCC projects were faced with having less funding than envisioned to meet the agreed-on objectives. At the time, at least six projects were scaled-back from original plans or supplemented by financing from other sources. In 2010, increased costs due to design changes and higher construction costs led to the reallocation of nearly $40 million for a Ghana transportation project. A reallocation of project resources was made unnecessary when bids on Tanzania's rural roads

---

[27] In August 2010, Senator Jim Webb raised the concern that some of these contracts had been won by Chinese government-owned firms. In a letter to the MCC, he argued that contracts awarded to Sinohydro Corporation for construction work in Mali and Tanzania supported Chinese foreign policy efforts to expand influence in Africa and harmed U.S. business. In September 2010, the MCC amended its procurement guidelines to prohibit contracts with state-owned enterprises (SOEs), except in the case of educational, research, and statistical units of government not formed for a commercial purpose. Its chief stated reason for making the change is to ensure a level playing field for competing firms. As of September 2010, $400 million of MCC contracts had gone to SOEs.

[28] Marco Bogran, Acting General Director, MCA-Honduras, and Ariane Gauchat, Associate Director, MCC, *MCC Hosts Public Event: Lessons Learned from MCC's First Compacts*, February 22, 2011, pages 9 and 32.

[29] For more details, see Office of Audit for the MCC, *Review of the Millennium Challenge Corporation's Compact Modifications*, M-000-12-006-S, July 16, 2012.

came in higher than budgeted, because the Tanzanian government committed funds to make up for the shortfall. The number of boreholes to be drilled under a rural water supply project in Mozambique was reduced from 600 to 300-400 because the amount allocated for construction was insufficient. Although the MCC is trying to address potential changes by requiring more frequent portfolio reviews and early identification of high risk projects, projects planned for a five-year life span are likely to undergo revision at some point. Changes in country policy performance, however, are less foreseeable and may carry more serious consequences. These are discussed below.

Compact Suspension and Termination

Throughout the entire process from candidacy to eligibility through development and implementation of a threshold program or compact, countries are expected to maintain a level of performance on the criteria reasonably close to that which brought them to their MCC threshold or compact-eligible status. On more than one occasion and for a variety of reasons, MCC programs have been suspended or terminated.

Section 611(a) of the Millennium Challenge Act of 2003 provides that, after consultation with MCC's Board of Directors (Board), the CEO may suspend or terminate assistance in whole or in part if the CEO determines that (1) the country or other entity receiving MCC aid is engaged in activities which are contrary to the national security interests of the United States; (2) the country or entity has engaged in a pattern of actions inconsistent with the criteria used to determine the eligibility of the country or entity; or (3) the country or entity has failed to adhere to its responsibilities under its compact. This policy applies to MCC assistance provided through a compact, for compact development and implementation, and assistance through a threshold agreement.[30] All compacts contain language providing that MCC may terminate the compact if the government engages in a pattern of action inconsistent with the criteria used to determine the eligibility of the country for assistance. This is the standard compact language that has been cited in most, if not all, prior MCC compact terminations.

In addition, all countries at all points of the process are affected by certain strictly applied foreign assistance restrictions in the Foreign Assistance Act of 1961 and in annual appropriations legislation. For example, restrictions on aid to countries whose governments are deposed by a military coup prevent countries from being considered for MCC candidacy, eligibility, or continued threshold or compact implementation.[31]

Application of legislative restrictions varies according to circumstances. The MCC has four steps available to it as responses to any perceived violations of its performance rules. It may warn a country of its concerns and potential consequences. It may place a program or part of a program on hold. These actions are both preliminary steps that can be taken by management without immediate concurrence of the Board. The two further steps, suspension and termination, must be made by the Board of Directors.

In all cases when some possible violation of MCC standards has been brought to the attention of the agency, the MCC Department of Policy and Evaluation conducts a review of the evidence and

---

[30] "MCC Policy on Suspension and Termination", available at http://www.mcc.gov/mcc/bm.doc/07-suspensionandterminationpolicy.pdf.

[31] Most recently, §7008 in P.L. 111-117, Division F, the State, Foreign Operations Appropriations, FY2010.

presents it with a recommendation to the Board. The Board does not uniformly follow the recommendation made. If a determination is made to hold, suspend, or terminate, it may be further determined to affect a whole or only part of the compact.

The MCC has suspended or terminated programs in the following cases (see **Appendix B** for details):

- Threshold programs have been suspended in Niger (December 2009, reinstated in June 2011), due to undemocratic actions taken by its leadership contrary to the MCC's governance criteria; suspended in Yemen (November 2005, reinstated February 2007, but never implemented) due to a pattern of deterioration in its performance criteria; and terminated in Mauritania (2008) due to aid prohibitions on governments deposed by a coup. See "Threshold Programs" section below for details.

- Compact eligibility was suspended in the Gambia (June 2006) because of "a disturbing pattern of deteriorating conditions" in half of the 16 qualifying factors.

- Portions of compacts have been terminated in Nicaragua (June 2009), because of the actions of the government inconsistent with the MCC eligibility criteria in the area of good governance; and in Honduras (September 2009), because of an undemocratic transfer of power contrary to the Ruling Justly criteria. The compact in Madagascar was terminated due to a military coup (May 2009). In Armenia (2008), MCC put a hold on a portion of the compact due to poor performance in a range of governance indicators, but the Board did not formally vote to suspend. The Mali compact, put on operational hold in March 2012 after a military coup, was terminated in August 2012.

- Most recently, in March 2012, the MCC Board suspended the Malawi compact. This followed the placing of an operational hold on the Malawi compact in July 2011, only a few months after the compact was signed, both steps taken as a result of a pattern of actions by the Malawi government "inconsistent with the democratic governance criteria" of the MCC. The Malawi suspension was lifted in June 2012 when democratic behavior significantly improved.

Inasmuch as there have been only 26 compacts and 23 threshold agreements to date, the number of holds, suspensions, or terminations suggests that the MCC takes seriously its legislative mandate by moving to address violations of its performance standards. These prior instances of MCC program suspension and termination indicate that the MCC is most likely to apply Section 611(a) in response to an undemocratic transfer/retention of power, a violation of the Ruling Justly eligibility criteria. The incidence of suspensions and terminations also suggests a weakness in the eligibility criteria that the new democratic rights "hard hurdle" for compact eligibility is meant to address. Despite these efforts by MCC, observers have noted instances in the past in which MCC has not taken action to restrict eligibility to countries with questionable records on political rights and civil liberties, for instance Jordan.[32] And, as noted above, a number of compact countries

---

[32] Freedom House, Press Release, "Millennium Challenge Corporation Should Hold Countries to Higher Standards of Democratic Governance, November 2, 2006, available at http://www.freedomhouse.org/template.cfm?page=70& release=435; Sheila Herrling, Steve Radelet, and Sarah Rose, "Will Politics Encroach in the MCA FY2007 Selection Round? The Cases of Jordan and Indonesia," Center for Global Development, October 30, 2006, http://www.cgdev.org.

have failed one or more of their qualifying indicators for one or more years in a row during the period of compact implementation.

Threshold Programs

In order to encourage non-qualifying countries to improve in weak areas, the MCC has helped governments that are committed to reform to strengthen their performance so that they would be more competitive for MCC funding in future years. Congress provided in the MCC authorizing legislation that not more than 10% of MCC appropriations could be used for such purposes, stating that the funding could be made available through USAID (§616 of P.L. 108-199).[33] Subsequent foreign operations appropriations made 10% of new MCC appropriations available for threshold assistance. Since the FY2012 appropriations, including FY2014, 5% is available for this purpose.

The FY2014 appropriations (P.L. 113-76) contain two new provisions specifically affecting threshold program eligibility. One prohibits a threshold program for countries that have already had a compact program. This provision is viewed by some as an after-the-fact response to the threshold eligibility granted Honduras for FY2012. Its program was signed in August 2013. The appropriations act also prohibits a new threshold program for any country not currently, in FY2014, a candidate country for MCC support. Tunisia, which had been granted threshold eligibility in September 2011, has graduated to upper-middle income status and, therefore, does not qualify as a candidate country in FY2014. If it were not for this new appropriations language, Tunisia might have received a threshold program funded with FY2011 appropriations, the year of its selection.

In the first part of 2010, the threshold program underwent an extensive review, the result of which has led to significant changes to the program. Up through mid-2010, the threshold programs sought chiefly to assist countries make policy reforms and institutional changes in areas where they failed to meet the MCC performance criteria with the stated goal of helping them improve those indicators.[34] Those countries deemed eligible for the program had to submit concept papers identifying where and why the country failed to pass specific indicators; make proposals for policy, regulatory, or institutional reforms that would improve the country's performance on these indicators; and note types of assistance, over a two-year maximum period, required to implement these reforms. If the MCC, in consultation with USAID, determined that the concept paper showed sufficient commitment to reform and a promise of success, the country would prepare a threshold country plan that specifically established a program schedule, the means to measure progress, and financing requirements, among other considerations. USAID was charged with overseeing the implementation of nearly all threshold country plans, including working with countries to identify appropriate implementing partners such as local, U.S., and international firms; NGOs; U.S. government agencies; and international organizations. Like regular MCC compacts, funding was not guaranteed for each country selected for the threshold program, but was based on the quality of the country plan.

---

[33] Assistance for threshold countries is authorized only for FY2004.

[34] Of the programs ongoing or completed, most have sought to improve country scores on the corruption indicator. Several countries had multiple objectives. Indonesia and Peru, for example, targeted both corruption and immunization indicators. Liberia's program focuses on girls' education and land rights. Timor-Leste targets corruption and childhood immunization.

Although eight threshold country programs were followed by compact eligibility, some Members of Congress and others raised concerns regarding the efficacy of threshold programs. It has been variously argued that two years is insufficient time to alter the indicators; that some countries passed the indicators before the threshold program could begin; that, by funding reform to improve an indicator, the threshold program undermines the principle that countries should themselves be responsible for reform and MCC eligibility; and that programs should focus on better preparing countries to implement compacts rather than on enabling them to qualify for eligibility.[35] In response to an explanatory statement accompanying the FY2009 Omnibus appropriations that suggested an assessment of the programs be undertaken before more are approved, the MCC did not select any new countries for threshold eligibility for FY2010 and did not request funding for the program in its FY2011 budget.

Following the threshold program review, the MCC briefed its board in June 2010 and announced in September 2010 a new approach to threshold programs. While maintaining the basic purpose of helping countries become compact-eligible as required by the authorizing language, the MCC no longer focuses on changing specific indicator scores. Rather, it focuses on constraints to economic growth, like those identified for compact countries, but maintains the former threshold program focus on reforming policies. Working on resolving constraints to growth is believed to have the benefit of helping MCC and the Board become more familiar with potential compact countries as well as of beginning to work on policy reforms for problem sectors that would likely be among the ones addressed in compact projects. For FY2014, both Guatemala and Nepal were reselected for the threshold program.

To date 24 threshold programs worth a total of over $500 million have been awarded to 22 countries, two of which have received second programs. Funding levels for threshold programs differ, ranging from $6.7 million for Guyana to $55 million for Indonesia. Currently, three countries are receiving threshold assistance: Honduras, Liberia, and Timor-Leste. Of those countries that have completed programs, Indonesia, Moldova, Burkina Faso, Jordan, Malawi, the Philippines, Tanzania, and Zambia have received compacts. The re-launch of Niger's previously suspended threshold program was ended when it was made compact eligible for FY2013.

Threshold countries are subject to the same performance rules as compact countries. Two countries—Mauritania and Yemen—have had their threshold eligibility terminated prior to program implementation, the former because of a coup and the latter due to deterioration in qualifying indicators.[36] One country—Niger—had its active threshold program suspended as its governance performance deteriorated.[37]

---

[35] One such critic, Sheila Herrling, has since become the MCC Vice President for Policy and Evaluation. See "Precedent-Setting Board Meeting for Team Obama," *MCA Monitor Blog*, June 9, 2009, Center for Global Development website http://blogs.cgdev.org/mca-monitor.

[36] Mauritania, made eligible in 2007, saw its eligibility terminated in 2008, prior to development of a threshold program agreement, due to aid prohibitions on governments deposed by a coup. Yemen, made threshold eligible in 2004, was suspended by the Board in November 2005, as a result of a consistent "pattern of deterioration" in its policy performance on selection criteria. Following a series of government reforms, Yemen's threshold status was reinstated in February 2007 and a threshold agreement valued at $20.6 million was approved in September 2007. In October 2007, however, the chair and ranking Member of the Senate Foreign Relations Committee noted their concern regarding the Yemen decision, in particular noting that, while Yemen had made reforms, its performance indicators had not yet shown improvement. The Members emphasized that, even if the MCC moved forward with the Yemen threshold program, "such compromises should never extend to the Compact program itself." In the end, implementation was postponed on October 27, 2007, pending a review, and its program has never been resumed.

[37] In September 2009, the MCC Board warned that Niger appeared to be moving away from its reform agenda, (continued...)

Select Issues

Concerns regarding the MCC have been expressed at various points in time on its level of funding, its operations, and its ability to ensure project sustainability; aspects of procurement; and the risk of corruption. These and other issues are discussed below.

Funding

When the MCC was proposed, it was expected that, within a few years, the level of funding would ramp up to about $5 billion per year. For a variety of reasons, not least of which is the limitation on available funding for foreign aid, the MCC never achieved anywhere near that level of funding. In fact, in most years since the MCC was established, its enacted appropriation has been well below the President's request.

Table 2. MCC Appropriations: FY2004-FY2015 Request

(in $ billions)

	FY04	FY05	FY06	FY07	FY08	FY09	FY10	FY11	FY12	FY13	FY14	FY15
Request	1.300	2.500	3.000	3.000	3.000	2.225	1.425	1.280	1.125	0.898	0.898	1.000
Enacted Approp	0.994	1.488	1.752	1.752	1.544	0.875	1.105	0.900	0.898	0.898	0.898	TBD
Post-Rescission Approp	0.989	1.480	1.751	1.746	1.484	0.871	1.081	0.898	0.898	0.853	0.898	TBD

Notes: P.L. 110-252 rescinded $58 million in FY2008 appropriation. P.L. 111-226 rescinded $50 million from unobligated amounts; MCC applied it to the 2004-2010 fiscal years. P.L. 112-10 includes an across-the-board 0.2% rescission in FY2011 appropriations. There was no rescission in FY2012. FY2013 level reflects both rescission and sequester. There was no rescission in FY2014. TBD= To Be Determined.

In determining the appropriation level, Congress has to weigh the benefits of the MCC program against all other foreign assistance programs as well as against other non-foreign policy needs. A consequence of diminished appropriations is that the agency may provide fewer compacts each year to fewer countries than originally anticipated. An additional impact may be that, if few compacts are offered annually, the incentive for countries to reform on their own in order to meet eligibility requirements—the so-called MCC effect—could be lost.

(...continued)

jeopardizing its $23 million threshold program. Niger's threshold program was suspended in December 2009 due to "political events that were inconsistent with the criteria used to determine eligibility for MCC assistance," when President Tandja dissolved parliament and dismissed the constitutional court after it ruled that a referendum to extend his presidential term was illegal. See MCC Congressional Notification, December 17, 2009, available at http://www.mcc.gov/mcc/bm.doc/cn-121709-niger.pdf. As noted above, in June 2011, following Niger's return to democratic rule, MCC announced it would reinstate the Niger program, and, in March 2012, $2 million was approved to enable completion of education activities under the original agreement. Further work on the program ended when Niger was made compact eligible in December 2012.

MCC Appropriations Request and Congressional Action for FY2015

On March 4, 2014, the Administration issued its FY2015 State, Foreign Operations budget request. It would provide $1 billion for the MCC, an 11% ($102 million) increase over the FY2014 appropriation. This amount, combined with as yet unobligated funds, is expected by the MCC to support first compacts with Liberia and Niger and second compacts with Ghana, Tanzania, and Morocco. Lesotho, also second compact-eligible, is not expected to offer its compact proposal in the near future.

On June 27, 2014, the House Appropriations Committee reported H.R. 5013, the FY2015 State, Foreign Operations appropriations, providing $898.2 million for the MCC, $101.8 million less than the Administration request and the same amount appropriated in FY2014.

On June 19, 2014, the Senate Appropriations Committee reported S. 2499, the FY2015 State, Foreign Operations appropriations, providing $901 million for the MCC, $99 million less than the Administration request and $2.8 million more than the amount appropriated in FY2014.

Opportunity, Growth and Security Initiative FY2015 Proposal

Associated with, but not included in, its FY2015 budget, the Administration proposed a $56 billion Opportunity, Growth and Security Initiative (OGSI) to support additional funding for domestic and international programs to be paid for through spending cuts and closure of tax loopholes identified in the Initiative. As part of this initiative, the Administration has proposed $350 million in additional funds for MCC activities in pending compacts. Of this amount, $50 million would supplement the road and power components of the Liberia compact, $125 million would support additional elements of the power sector in the Ghana II compact, $125 million would assist access to electric power in rural areas under the Tanzania II compact, and $50 million would support due diligence activities for new compacts. OGSI funding is not included in FY2015 budget request figures.

Neither House nor Senate versions of the FY2015 State, Foreign Operations appropriations bills address the OGSI request.

MCC Appropriations Request and Congressional Action for FY2014

On April 10, 2013, the Administration issued its FY2014 State, Foreign Operations budget request. It sought $898.2 million for the MCC in FY2014, the same level as appropriated in FY2011 and FY2012, and $45.47 million more than the agency-estimated post-sequester FY2013 level, a 5% increase from the FY2013 agency estimate.

In June 2013, both House and Senate Appropriations Committees reported out their versions of the FY2014 State, Foreign Operations appropriations. The House bill, H.R. 2855 (H.Rept. 113-185), provided $701.9 million to the MCC, an 18% cut from the FY2013 level. The committee noted that despite the substantial decrease, a response to budget concerns, it continued to strongly support the agency. The House report voiced concern regarding weak judicial systems and corruption in compact countries, suggesting the MCC review its response to such problems and report to the committee. It also continued to expect MCC to support economic growth and to note the expected economic rate of return for each line item of compact in notification of new compacts. The committee requested a report on second compacts, including the level of matching funds from recipient governments.

The Senate bill, S. 1372 (S.Rept. 113-81), provided $899 million for the MCC, a 5% increase over the FY2013 level. The Senate report raised concerns about the methodology for constructing the corruption eligibility indicator, specifically noting that second compacts and threshold programs have gone to countries, such as Honduras and El Salvador, with significant corruption. It included legislative language in its bill that requires that second compact countries significantly improve their corruption indicator. It also prohibits threshold programs to countries that already had compacts. The committee requested a report on how compacts are aligned with U.S. strategic interests regionally and with other U.S. assistance programs, how they are sustainable, and whether lessons learned since the MCC was launched indicate any need for change in the MCC model.

On October 17, 2013, the President signed P.L. 113-46, the Continuing Appropriations Act, 2014, providing FY2014 MCC funding at the FY2013 post-sequester level of $853 million. The provision providing this appropriation expired on January 15, 2014.

On January 17, 2014, the President signed P.L. 113-76, the Consolidated Appropriations Act, 2014, providing the MCC with $898.2 million in FY2014, matching the Administration request and a 5% increase over the FY2013 post-sequester level. The legislation also expressly prohibited threshold programs to countries that previously had compacts and to countries not currently MCC candidates.

The statement of conferees attached to the legislation notes that Senate and House committee report language, noted above, should be followed unless expressly refuted by the conferees. The statement repeated much of the Senate language regarding the anti-corruption indicator, asking the MCC to improve its eligibility criteria in this area. It also indicated that its prohibition on threshold programs to non-current MCC candidates, included Tunisia, and suggested that providing aid to countries not meeting MCC criteria would undermine the integrity of the MCC model.

Authorizing Legislation and MCC Reform

Congress has not enacted a new funding authorization since the original MCC legislation in 2004 authorized "such sums as may be necessary" for FY2004 and FY2005. Appropriations bills, however, routinely waive the requirement of authorization of appropriations for foreign aid programs, as the Continuing Appropriations Act 2014 (P.L. 113-46, Division A, §113) did in the case of FY2014 unauthorized foreign aid program appropriations, including those for MCC.

Periodically, the MCC has asked Congress to approve new authorization language, but while various proposals were considered and approved by the authorizing committees, most were attached to broader legislation that was not successful on the floor.[38] In the FY2015 budget, MCC has requested the following provisions, all of which were requested as well in FY2014:

---

[38] Significant MCC policy language, including that requested by the agency, was offered in the 109th Congress (2006): H.R. 4014, reported by the House International Relations Committee (H.Rept. 109-563); in the 111th Congress (2010), S. 2971, reported by the Senate Foreign Relations Committee (S.Rept. 111-301); and in the 112th Congress (2011), S. 1426, a Foreign Relations Authorization bill introduced by Senator Kerry, and H.R. 2583, a Foreign Relations (continued...)

- allow an MCC compact to exceed five years in length, up to one additional year, if it cannot be completed on time. This provision was deemed necessary by MCC in view of the difficulties that recipient countries may have in implementing complex projects within a limited timeframe. It would be used only in "exceptional circumstances."

- allow MCC private sector Board members to remain on the Board for one year after expiration of their term or until, in the case of members serving their first terms, they have been confirmed for a second term, or their successor has been confirmed. This request reflects the long-standing vacancies of private sector positions on the Board and the possible failure to achieve a quorum as was the case in December 2010 when FY2011 compact-eligible countries could not be selected.

- delete a provision in the authorization, Section 604(b)(2)(B), for an interim CEO as a presidential memorandum on May 21, 2012, provides an order of succession.

A number of provisions previously requested by MCC were not requested again this year. Among these is a provision to allow concurrent compacts (more than one at the same time), in order to give the MCC flexibility to do smaller, staggered projects, instead of wrapping them all in one compact. Also absent in this year's authorization request is language (discussed in the "Identification of Candidate Countries" section above) that has appeared regularly in recent appropriations acts, including FY2014 (P.L. 113-76), and, due to its importance to MCC, presumably is anticipated to continue in future appropriations. This language makes the eligibility pool more stable by redefining low- and lower-middle income status for funding purposes (the bottom 75 countries become low-income) and requiring, for purposes of compact eligibility, that countries transitioning from low-income to lower-middle income status or vice versa would retain their former classification for three years. The MCC has not indicated a reason for neglecting to request these provisions in the form of authorization language this year.

In addition to MCC-supported legislative proposals, various concerns expressed in Congress or by other observers in the past decade suggest several areas of MCC operations that might invite scrutiny for possible reforms and the legislative language supporting them. These would include language better "aligning" MCC programs with U.S. foreign policy interests, limiting the size of compacts, supporting alternate methods of compact support such as cash transfers, establishing new or changed qualifying factors, strengthening democracy language in the qualifying factors and the role of civil society in compact development and implementation, reinforcing the anti-corruption language (the pass/fail indicator is not embodied in the legislation), supporting and funding post-compact evaluations, authorizing the recent changes to the threshold program, and specifying new requirements, including possible tougher standards, for second compacts.

Compact Outcomes and Impact

The MCC places considerable weight on demonstrating results. During project development, it predicts a set of outcomes that help determine which projects will be funded. During implementation, it gathers data to establish baselines and monitor performance. And, at project

---

(...continued)

Authorization bill reported by the House Foreign Affairs Committee (H.Rept. 112-223).

completion, it supports independent evaluations of achievements. It promises to release these findings to the public, regardless of the results, with the intention of improving the agency's performance in meeting its purpose of reducing poverty through economic growth.

In the MCC's first years of existence, however, some observers complained about the lack of measurable results.[39] One reason for the seeming absence of results was the slow speed of compact implementation. A second was that the first compact programs only ended in late 2010, and it was reasonable to expect that it would be some time after project closures before a serious analysis of actual impacts could be undertaken. Nonetheless, as the delay continued, a degree of impatience was not unfounded. Finally, two years after the initial compacts ended, the first evaluations were released in October 2012, focusing on five farmer training projects. About 120 other independent impact evaluations are promised over the next few years.[40] As of early July 2014, seven evaluations of threshold programs—representing about one-third of the completed programs—have been posted on the MCC website.[41] Eleven compact project evaluations have also been published on the site, but, as each of the 16 completed compacts encompasses multiple sub-projects, it is hard to say what proportion of the total universe of projects have been examined to date.

In fact, the agency argues that it has been producing results of varying kinds since it was launched. First is the impact made by the MCC process itself. Under the so-called "MCC effect," countries are said to be establishing reforms in an effort to qualify under the 20 performance indicators. Yemen has been cited in this regard because, following its suspension from the threshold program in 2005, it approved a number of reforms to address indicators where its performance had lapsed (and subsequently was reinstated and then later suspended for different reasons). Niger passed the Natural Resources Protection indicator in FY2013 as a consequence of establishing a large new protected area. House and Senate-approved resolutions in 2007 (H.Res. 294 and S.Res. 103) noted the role the MCC played in encouraging Lesotho to adopt legislation improving the rights of married women. It can also be argued that the establishment of local compact implementation mechanisms—the MCAs—has served a capacity building function and influenced some governments' procurement policies.

Second, assistance program inputs—financing, technical expertise, construction, etc.—produce outputs. The MCC notes that its programs have trained 210,851 farmers, built 830 educational facilities, completed 1,712 kilometers of roads, and constructed 11,756 sanitation systems.

Third, some of these outputs have led to medium-term outcomes, such as an increase by 20,000 in the number of new registered businesses in Albania as a result of administrative reforms made in business licensing under its threshold program. An independent analysis of the Burkina Faso threshold program found that construction of 132 primary schools led to increased enrollment for both boys and girls by about 20% and for girls over boys by 5%.[42] Among the outcomes of its

---

[39] For example, the Senate Appropriations Committee report (S.Rept. 110-425) on its version of the FY2009 State/Foreign Operations appropriations explained a proposed cut to the MCC by noting the small compact disbursement rate (4% of total compact funding at the time) and the lack of tangible results to date as factors. The committee stated its intention to support future compacts "if current country compacts are shown to be cost effective and achieving results."

[40] MCC CEO Daniel Yohannes, MCC Quarterly Town Hall Meeting, September 14, 2012, based on transcript.

[41] At http://data.mcc.gov/evaluations/index.php/catalog.

[42] MCC Public Board Meeting, June 11, 2009. Mathematica Policy Research, Inc., *Impact Evaluation of Burkina Faso's BRIGHT Program*, March 2009.

Port of Cotonou modernization project under the Benin compact, according to MCC, are annual savings of $2.1 million in dredging and maintenance costs and a decrease in average customs clearance time.[43]

The fourth and perhaps most important measure of MCC activity is the long-term impact compacts can have on poverty reduction through increased incomes among poor people, the legislative mandate of the agency. Independent post-compact impact evaluations are meant to explore the relationship between an MCC investment and such an outcome, if any, so as to provide lessons for future compacts. As noted, the first such impact evaluations were published in October 2012. Examining farmer training programs conducted in five compact countries, the evaluations affirmed that the *average* of individual outputs anticipated for a country, such as the number of farmers trained and hectares under production with MCC support, met or exceeded their targets in all five cases (although for two countries a number of indicators had no targets). While the evaluations found increases in *farm* income in three countries—no measurements could be undertaken in a fourth country—in no case was it able to identify increases in *household* incomes. This finding may be due to a household reallocating other income sources to farming or because household income is too difficult to measure. In any case, MCC is looking for alternative methods for measuring household income for application to future compacts.

Some concerns have been raised by GAO regarding the possible outputs and impacts of MCC compacts. A 2007 GAO report highlighted a concern that, in the case of Vanuatu, projected impacts had been overstated. The GAO noted that the MCC estimated a rise from 2005 per capita income in Vanuatu of about 15% ($200) by 2015 when the data suggest it would rise by 4.6%. Although the MCC states that the compact would benefit 65,000 poor, rural inhabitants, the data, according to the GAO, do not establish the extent of benefit to the rural poor. Further, the MCC projections assume continued maintenance of projects following completion, whereas the experience of previous donors is that such maintenance has been poor.[44] The MCC response was that, although there may be varying views on the degree of benefit, both agencies agree that the underlying data show that the compact would help Vanuatu address poverty reduction.[45]

A September 2012 GAO report called into question the quality of data used to determine beneficiary numbers in seven transportation projects, pointing to mistakes made in formulas used, a failure to apply a methodology to all compacts, and a failure to update numbers in public documents.[46] A June 2012 GAO report questioned the quality of work done on a road construction project in Georgia and noted an array of problems that have kept part of a port constructed by MCC in Benin from full operability.[47] Sustainability concerns were raised for both projects (see below for discussion).

---

[43] MCC, *Fact Sheet: MCC's Continuum of Results*, May 23, 2012.

[44] Government Accountability Office, *Millennium Challenge Corporation: Vanuatu Compact Overstates Projected Program Impact*, July 2007, GAO-07-909.

[45] Testimony of Rodney Bent before the House Committee on Foreign Affairs, Subcommittee on Asia, the Pacific, and the Global Environment, July 26, 2007.

[46] GAO, *Millennium Challenge Corporation: Results of Transportation Infrastructure Projects in Seven Countries*, 12-631, September 2012.

[47] GAO, *Millennium Challenge Corporation: Georgia and Benin Transportation Infrastructure Projects Varied in Quality and May Not Be Sustainable*, 12-630, June 2012.

Ensuring Sustainability

An important factor in assessing the success of development assistance programs, one strongly emphasized by the MCC, is the extent to which assistance efforts are sustainable after donor support ends. This question is of particular significance in the case of the MCC as most of its assistance is in the form of infrastructure, which developing countries, historically, have had difficulty maintaining due to lack of funds for physical upkeep or lack of trained technical personnel for regular maintenance.

The MCC often conditions compact aid on country adoption of policy reforms that enhance sustainability. In Tanzania, for example, the government electric power services were required to reform their tariff schedules in order to fully recover their costs, and, in those countries with road projects, provisions have been included to ensure establishment or improvement of a road fund to pay for upkeep.

GAO reports on completed compacts, however, have questioned the effectiveness of MCC sustainability efforts in the cases it examined. In Cape Verde, the road fund reportedly met only half of maintenance requirements, and water fees, established to fund infrastructure maintenance for the watershed and agricultural support project, were not being collected in one of the three watersheds. In Honduras, a required increase in the national road maintenance budget was believed to be insufficient to meet needs and was intended to address all roads, not just those funded by the MCC. Further, farm-to-market roads provided under the Honduras compact were the responsibility of municipalities that, reportedly, lacked equipment, expertise, and funds for road maintenance.[48] GAO noted that, while the MCC included conditions precedent in its compact with Georgia requiring the government to maintain a level of funding for road maintenance, the government "shows limited ability to keep the road operational and well maintained." It has also questioned the ability of Benin's port authority to operate key components.[49]

Corruption

In 2014, appropriators in both House and Senate Committee reports on their versions of the FY2015 State, Foreign Operations appropriations (H.Rept. 113-499 and S.Rept. 113-195), expressed continued concern regarding corruption in MCC compact countries. In 2013, each committee had addressed the issue and the statement of conferees on the final FY2014 Consolidated Appropriations (P.L. 113-76) voiced concern over the utility of the "control of corruption" indicator as a reflection of adherence to rule of law, including enforcement of private sector contracts. It directed the MCC to improve its eligibility criteria in this area. This follows suggestions from Congress in previous years that the MCC should take the issue of corruption

---

[48] Government Accountability Office, *Millennium Challenge Corporation: Compacts in Cape Verde and Honduras Achieved Reduced Targets*, GAO-11-728, July 2011.

[49] GAO, *Millennium Challenge Corporation: Georgia and Benin Transportation Infrastructure Projects Varied in Quality and May Not be Sustainable*, 12-630, June 2012, p. 33 and p. 47. Sustainability concerns have also been raised in 2012 MCC Office of the Inspector General reports regarding a fruit tree productivity project in Morocco and a Senegalese road project. See Office of the Inspector General, USAID, *Management Challenges Identified by the Inspector General, November 26, 2013*, in MCC, *Agency Financial Report, FY2013*. The USAID Inspector General also acts in that capacity for the MCC.

more into account in judging compact country behavior.[50] In response to the FY2014 statement of conferees, the MCC Board noted its commitment to improving measures of corruption at its March 2014 meeting.

With developing countries themselves implementing MCC-funded programs, corruption is a major concern of the MCC, in the selection process, in threshold programs, and in compact implementation. Aiming to safeguard U.S. aid dollars, MCC programs are designed to prevent corrupt contracting. Among other things, MCC requires a transparent and competitive process and mandates separation of technical and financial elements of a bid. The MCC reviews each decision made by the procurement entity and must register approval for many of them, and it provides funds directly to contractors rather than through the government implementing entity. MCC argues that, in following this process, recipient governments learn how to do procurement in a corruption-free way.

The degree to which a country controls corruption is one of the performance indicators that help determine whether a country should be eligible for compact funding. In fact, it is a "pass-fail" indicator. Passing the indicator, however, does not mean there is little or no corruption—an unrealistic expectation for most developing countries. It only demonstrates that a country's performance is above the median relative to other countries at the same economic level. Further, as suggested in the discussion of country selection, the MCC board does not depend on indicator scores alone to determine the selection process. These scores change from year to year, depending on fresh data and the relative scores of competing countries. Taking this into account, the MCC board uses discretion by looking at a number of factors, including the many underlying data sources that make up indicators, as well as recent steps taken by the government in question to address corruption (or, in some cases, recent increased allegations of corruption). Accordingly, a country can be selected that technically falls near or below the median if mitigating factors occur. Alternatively, countries that pass the corruption indicator may be the subject of intense debate over incidences of alleged corruption. Because of data lags, countries passing the indicator may fail a year or two later, once a compact is in place. This can be true of all the indicators, particularly when a country "graduates" into a higher income category, thereby changing the medians. The MCC attempts to address this concern by looking for a pattern of behavior on the part of the government in order to judge the severity of any proposed corrective action. In the FY2014 compact eligibility selection process, two countries that had been selected in FY2013— Benin and Sierra Leone—were dropped from compact consideration due to their failing grades on the "control of corruption" indicator.

---

[50] During hearings in 2010 with the MCC CEO, the House State, Foreign Operations Appropriations Subcommittee chair and ranking Member raised concerns regarding the absence of termination guidelines based on a pattern of corruption. (Hearing with Daniel Yohannes, MCC CEO, April 14, 2010.) In 2009 and 2010, several Members of Congress noted their concern regarding provision of MCC funding to corrupt countries. ("For Senegal: U.S. Aid, 164-ft. Statue," *The Washington Times*, August 16, 2010.) Specifically, they each referred to the case of Senegal, whose leader installed a monument to the country's independence estimated to cost between $24 million and $70 million. The $540 million compact with Senegal was signed in September 2009. Despite corruption reports, Senegal scored in the 74th percentile of the FY2011 Control of Corruption indicator formulated by the World Bank. The MCC said it had looked at but found no pattern of corrupt behavior since signing the Senegal compact that would justify suspending or closing the compact program. It notified the Senegalese government that any decline in policy performance, regardless of indicator scores, could jeopardize the compact.

Appendix A. MCC Compacts at a Glance

Country	Compact Signed	Compact Size (millions)	Entry Into Force	Compact Completion	Compact Focus
Armenia	Mar. 27, 2006	$236 5 years	Sept. 29, 2006	September 2011	Agriculture/irrigation Rural roads
Benin	Feb. 22, 2006	$307 5 years	Oct. 6, 2006	October 2011	Land and property Financial services Judicial improvement Port rehab
Burkina Faso	July 14, 2008	$481 5 years	July 31, 2009		Rural land governance Agriculture Roads Education
Cape Verde I	July 4, 2005	$110 5 years	Oct. 17, 2005	October 2010	Agriculture Transport/roads Private sector
Cape Verde II	Feb. 10, 2012	$66.2 5 years	Nov. 30, 2012		Water and sanitation Land management
El Salvador I	Nov. 29, 2006	$461 5 years	Sept. 20, 2007	September 2012	Education Transport/roads Small business/farm development
El Salvador II	Board Approved Sept 2013	$277 5 years	—		Investment Climate Reform Education Logistical infrastructure: Road and border crossing
Georgia I	Sept. 12, 2005	$295 5 years	April 7, 2006	April 2011	Infrastructure/gas Transport/roads Agriculture/business
Georgia II	July 26, 2013	$140 5 years	—		Education: Infrastructure and training Education: Workforce development Education: Sci and tech higher ed
Ghana	August 1, 2006	$547 5 years	Feb. 16, 2007	February 2012	Agriculture Transport Rural development
Honduras	June 13, 2005	$215 5 years	Sept. 29, 2005	September 2010	Agriculture Transport/roads
Indonesia	Nov. 18, 2011	$600 5 years	April 2, 2013		Energy and resource management Health and nutrition Public procurement
Jordan	Oct. 25, 2010	$275.1 5 years	Dec. 13, 2011		Clean water and sanitation
Lesotho	July 23, 2007	$362.6 5 years	Sept. 17, 2008	September 2013	Water sector Health sector Private sector
Madagascar (terminated May	April 18, 2005	$110 4 years	July 27, 2005	May 2009	Land titling/agriculture Financial sector

Country	Compact Signed	Compact Size (millions)	Entry Into Force	Compact Completion	Compact Focus
2009)					
Malawi	April 7, 2011	$350.7 5 years	Sept. 20, 2013		Electric power
Mali (terminated August 2012)	Nov. 13, 2006	$460.8 5 years	Sept. 17, 2007	August 2012	Irrigation Transport/airport Industrial park
Moldova	Jan. 22, 2010	$262 5 years	Sept. 1, 2010		Agriculture Roads
Mongolia	Oct. 22, 2007	$285 5 years	Sept. 17, 2008	September 2013	Transport/rail Property ights Voc ed Health
Morocco	August 31, 2007	$697.5 5 years	Sept. 15, 2008	September 2013	Agriculture/fisheries Artisan crafts Financial serv/enterprise support
Mozambique	July 13, 2007	$506.9 5 years	Sept. 22, 2008	September 2013	Water and sanitation Transport Land tenure/agri
Namibia	July 28, 2008	$305 5 years	Sept. 16, 2009		Education Tourism Agriculture
Nicaragua	July 14, 2005	$175 5 years	May 26, 2006	May 2011	Land titling/agriculture Transport roads
Philippines	Sept. 23, 2010	$434 5 years	May 25, 2011		Revenue reform Community dev Road rehab
Senegal	Sept. 16, 2009	$540 5 years	Sept. 23, 2010		Roads Irrigation
Tanzania	Feb. 17, 2008	$698 5 years	Sept. 15, 2008	September 2013	Transport/roads, airport Energy Water
Vanuatu	March 2, 2006	$66 5 years	April 28, 2006	April 2011	Transport rehab Public works dept.
Zambia	May 10, 2012	$354.8 5 years	Nov. 15, 2013		Water supply and sanitation

Source: MCC.

Appendix B. Compact Descriptions and Status

Descriptions and key developments in the 27 signed and one Board-approved compacts undertaken by the MCC since 2004 are provided below in alphabetical order. Compact funding totals include administrative and monitoring costs.

Armenia

The five-year, $236 million compact, completed in September 2011, concentrated on the agricultural sector, investing in the rehabilitation of rural roads ($67 million) and improving irrigation ($146 million). When launched, the program anticipated that it would benefit about 750,000 people, 75% of Armenia's rural population, by improving 943 kilometers of rural roads and increasing the amount of land under irrigation by 40%.

Misgivings were raised both prior to and during implementation of the Armenia compact. In September 2005, during compact development, the MCC expressed concerns with Armenian officials regarding slippage on two of the governance indicators and matters raised by international groups concerning political rights and freedoms in the country. Moreover, the MCC Board delayed final approval of the compact following the November 27, 2005, constitutional referendum, after allegations of fraud, mismanagement, limited access by the press, and abuse of individuals were raised. In signing the compact on March 27, 2006, the MCC issued a cautionary note, signaling that Armenia must maintain its commitment to the performance indicators or risk suspension or termination of the compact. On March 11, 2008, the MCC issued a warning that assistance might be suspended or terminated in response to the government's actions, including the imposition of a state of emergency and restrictions on press freedoms.[51] In the autumn of 2008, the Armenian government used $17 million of its own funds to begin a road segment when there was some question of whether the MCC would continue its support. In December 2008, then-MCC CEO Danilovich noted that Armenia had since moved forward on a number of reforms addressing MCC concerns and he expected MCC support to resume in the spring of 2009.[52] However, on March 11, 2009, the MCC Board of Directors declined to lift the funding hold for the rural roads component of the Armenia compact until an interim review session could be held prior to its normal June 2009 meeting in order to assess the status of democratic governance in Armenia. On June 10, 2009, the MCC Board allowed the hold to continue on financial support for the roads project. One board member noted that the hold on funding was, in effect, a termination, as the work, if reapproved, could not be completed within the compact lifespan.[53]

Benin

The five-year, $307 million compact, completed in October 2011, focused on four sectors—land rights, reducing the time and cost of obtaining property title; financial services, helping micro, small, and medium-sized businesses; justice reform, assisting the judicial system's capacity to resolve business and investment claims; and market access, improving the Port of Cotonou. When

---

[51] See letters of John Danilovich to Armenia President Robert Kocharyan on December 16, 2005 and March 11, 2008 on MCC website.

[52] MCC, Public Outreach Meeting Transcript, December 12, 2008, p. 12.

[53] Lorne Craner at Public Outreach Meeting, June 11, 2009.

launched, the compact's goal was to benefit 5 million people, bringing 250,000 of the population out of poverty by 2015.

Burkina Faso

The five-year, $480.9 million compact has four elements. A rural land governance project ($59.9 million) will focus on improving legal and institutional approaches to rural land issues, including registration and land use management. An agriculture project ($141.9 million) will target water management and irrigation, diversified agriculture, and access to rural finance in specific regions of the country. A roads project ($194.1 million) will improve rural roads. The education effort ($28.8 million) will build on the country's MCC threshold program and construct additional classrooms and provide daily meals to children. The education project will be administered by USAID.

Cape Verde I

The five-year, $110 million compact, completed in October 2010, focused largely on improving the country's investment climate, transportation networks, and agriculture productivity. The program's goal was to increase the annual income in Cape Verde by at least $10 million.

The compact evolved around three projects. In support of private sector development, $2.1 million and additional participation with the International Finance Corporation was used to remove constraints to private sector investment by creating a commercial credit information bureau and to stimulate other reforms. The MCC invested $83.2 million primarily for port construction to help link the nine inhabited islands and roads and bridges to improve transportation links to social services, employment opportunities, and local markets. By investing $11.4 million to increase the collection and distribution of rainfall water and strengthen agribusiness services, including access to credit, the project hoped to increase agricultural production and double the household income of farmers.

Cape Verde is the first compact country to be made eligible for a second compact.

Cape Verde II

Cape Verde's $66.2 million second compact will address two issues impeding economic growth. A water and sanitation project ($41 million) aims to reform the regulatory regime and utility structure and provide capital infrastructure improvements. A land management project ($17 million) is expected to induce legal reforms and the clarification of property rights. Meeting an MCC requirement for second compacts, the government of Cape Verde will contribute an additional 15% of total costs toward project implementation.

El Salvador I

The five-year, $461 million compact, completed in September 2012, addressed economic growth and poverty reduction concerns in El Salvador's northern region, where more than half the population lives below the poverty line. Education as well as water and sanitation, and electricity supply ($95.1 million); support for poor farmers and small and medium-sized business ($87.5

million); and transportation, including roads ($233.6 million), were the chief elements of program.

El Salvador II

In September 2013, the MCC Board approved a $277 million five-year second compact with El Salvador. The compact consists of three projects. One will address constraints in the investment climate by developing an independent institution seeking regulatory improvement and will build the capacity of government to partner with the private sector in public service delivery ($42.4 million). A second project will focus on development of human capital, reforming education policy to increase school hours and strengthen the curriculum, and would also address skills needed by the labor market ($100.7 million). The third project will meet identified infrastructure needs—expansion of an important roadway and border crossing improvements related to commerce ($109.6 million). El Salvador will contribute $88 million to project implementation.

Georgia I

The $395 million, five-year agreement with Georgia ended in April 2011. It focused on reducing poverty and promoting economic growth in areas outside of the capital, where over half the population lives in poverty. The compact was divided into two projects. The first and the largest component ($311.7 million) concentrated on infrastructure rehabilitation, including roads, the north-south gas pipeline, water supply networks, and solid waste facilities. The Enterprise Development Project ($47.5 million) financed an investment fund aimed at providing risk capital and technical assistance to small and medium-sized businesses, and support farmers and agribusinesses that produce commodities for the domestic market.

The program expected to reduce the incidence of poverty by 12% in the Samtskhi-Javakheti region; provide direct benefits to 500,000 people and indirectly benefit over 25% of Georgia's population; reduce the travel time by 43% to Tbilisi, the capital, from regional areas, thereby cutting transportation costs for farmers, businesses, and individuals needing health and other social services; and lower the risk of a major gas pipeline accident and improve the reliability of heat and electricity to over 1 million Georgians.

The original compact agreement totaled $295 million, but, on September 4, 2008, the Bush Administration proposed a $1 billion aid initiative for Georgia, of which one component was adding $100 million to the existing compact. An amendment to the compact was signed on November 20, 2008, making the total $395 million. Complementing or completing projects begun in the original compact, it was directed at road projects, water and sanitation facilities, and a natural gas storage facility.

Georgia II

The five-year $140 million second compact would address education concerns in three ways. One project seeks to improve the quality education through infrastructure improvements and training of educators ($76.5 million). A second project will focus on meeting labor market needs through skills development ($16 million). A third project will modernize the teaching of science, technology, and math ($30 million).

Ghana

The five-year, $547 million compact, which ended in February 2012, focused on agriculture and rural development. Poverty rates in the three targeted geographic areas were above 40%. The agriculture component ($241 million) provided training for farmer-based organizations, improved irrigation, greater access to credit, and rehabilitated local roads. The transport component ($143 million) sought to reduce transport costs to farmers by improving key roads, such as the one between the capital and the airport, and an important ferry service. Rural development programs ($101 million) constructed and rehabilitated education, water, and electric facilities, among other activities.

Ghana has been selected as eligible for a second compact.

Honduras

The five-year, $205 million (originally $215 million) compact with Honduras, completed in September 2010, focused on two objectives—rural development and transportation. The rural development project, representing $68.3 million of the compact, assisted small and medium-size farmers to enhance their business skills and to transition from the production of basic grains to more high-value horticultural crops, such as cucumbers, peppers, and tomatoes. The project provided farmers with the appropriate infrastructure and necessary training for producing and marketing these different crops. More than 7,000 farmers were trained, of which 6,029 significantly increased production of horticulture crops. About 422 kilometers of rural roads were also upgraded, helping farmers transport their goods to markets at a lower cost. The original objective was 1,500 kilometers, but increased construction costs limited that figure.

The transportation project, totaling $119.2 million of the compact, sought to improve the CA-5 major highway linking Honduran Atlantic and Pacific ports and major production centers in Honduras, El Salvador, and Nicaragua. Almost 50 kilometers of the CA-5 were completed of 107 originally planned and 45 of 68 kilometers in secondary roads before an undemocratic change in government contrary to MCC's Ruling Justly criteria—the removal of President Zelaya from office by a coalition of civilian and military institutions—led to the September 9, 2009, MCC termination of these two planned activities in the transportation sector. The termination affected about $10 million in funding, including $4 million for the CA-5 road project. Already contractually obligated programs were continued.[54]

Honduras has not been selected as eligible for a second compact due to concerns over governance.

Indonesia

The five-year, $600 million compact has three projects. A Green Prosperity project ($332.5 million) will provide technical expertise and funding for renewable energy and natural resource management efforts that aim to raise household incomes. A community-based health and nutrition project ($131.5 million) is aimed at reducing stunting, from which more than one-third of

---

[54] See MCC Congressional Notification, September 17, 2009, at http://www.mcc.gov/mcc/bm.doc/cn-091709-honduras.pdf.

Indonesia's children suffer. A public procurement reform project ($50 million) seeks to implement practices that will counter fraud, waste, and abuse that results in the loss of billions of dollars annually.

Jordan

The five-year, $275.1 million compact is solely aimed at the water sector. In the governorate of Zarqa, it will reduce water loss by rehabilitating the water supply and distribution network from reservoir to household ($102.5 million) and will improve the sewage system by replacing or rehabilitating sewage lines ($58.22 million). In a partnership with the private sector, the compact will also expand a wastewater treatment plant originally built by USAID ($93.03 million).

Lesotho

The five-year, $362.6 million compact, completed in September 2013, had three elements. A water sector project ($164 million) focused on both industrial, supporting garment and textile operations, and domestic needs. It also supported a national watershed management and wetlands conservation plan. A health project ($122.4 million) sought to strengthen the health care infrastructure, including renovation of up to 150 health centers, improved management of up to 14 hospital out-patient departments, construction and equipping of a central laboratory, and improved housing for medical staff and training for nurses. A private sector development project ($36.1 million) addressed a wide range of legal and administrative obstacles to increased private sector activity, including development of land policy and administration authority, implementation of a new payments and settlement system, and improvement of case management of commercial courts.

Lesotho has been selected as eligible for a second compact.

Madagascar

The Madagascar compact, MCC's first signed agreement, started out as a four-year, $110 million program, was extended to five years because of start-up delays, and then terminated prematurely because of a coup. The project had three objectives: (1) to increase land titling and land security ($36 million), (2) to expand the financial sector and increase competition ($36 million), and (3) to improve agricultural production technologies and market capacity in rural areas ($17 million). After restoring 149,000 land rights documents, digitizing another 128,000, formalizing land rights for 12,800 families, constructing two new bank branches, and providing agriculture technical assistance to 34,450 farmers and 290 small businesses and farmers associations, the compact ended in May 2009, with little more than a year remaining in the compact's five-year span and $88 million of the $110 million project committed.

Malawi

The five-year, $350.7 million Malawi compact, signed in April 2011, focuses on just one sector—electric power. The program aims to reduce power outages, reduce costs to business and homes, and improve the economic environment. One element will upgrade and modernize generation and distribution capacity ($283 million); another will reform electric power supply institutions in the country ($25.7 million). In July 2011, the compact, which had not yet entered into force, was put on operational hold in response to concerns raised by several anti-democratic actions taken by the government, including suppression of the media and prevention of peaceful protests. In March 2012, the compact was suspended in view of the continuing pattern of actions "inconsistent" with good governance. On June 26, 2012, the MCC reinstated its compact with Malawi. A change in the country's leadership and subsequent steps to restore democratic society led the Board to change its position.

Mali

The compact was due for completion in September 2012. However, on March 22, 2012, the MCC announced it was halting its operations in Mali, following a military coup. The compact was formally terminated in August 2012.

The five-year, $461 million compact emphasized an increase in agricultural production and expansion of trade. About half the funds ($234.6 million) supported a major irrigation project, including modernization of infrastructure and improvements in land tenure. Improvements in the airport ($89.6 million) targeted both passenger and freight operations. Due to rising construction costs and changes in currency valuations, $94.6 million in funds originally intended for construction of an industrial park at the airport were reallocated to the airport project. The early termination left some components uncompleted, including the airport terminal building and half of a 80 km road.

Moldova

The five-year, $262 million compact addresses agriculture and roads. On the agriculture side, $101.77 million will be provided to repair large irrigation systems supporting high-value fruits and vegetables, to support the legal transfer for these systems to water user organizations, and to facilitate financing facilities for farmers and entrepreneurs. USAID will provide technical assistance to improve market access for high-value agriculture. The compact will also provide $132.84 million to repair a major bridge and highway leading toward Ukraine, facilitating commercial traffic between the two countries.

Mongolia

Mongolia's compact was completed in September 2013. The most significant part of the original five-year, $285 million compact was intended to stimulate economic growth by refurbishing the rail system, including infrastructure and management ($188.38 million). However, in April 2009, the government of Mongolia informed the MCC that it would not be able to implement the $188 million rail component of its compact, because Russian members of the joint Mongolian-Russian rail company would not allow an audit of the company.

The MCC decided to use $52 million of this amount to expand the three other original projects in the compact. These included support for improvements in the property registration and titling system ($23.06 million) and the vocational education system ($25.51 million), and an attempt to reform the health system to better address non-communicable diseases and injuries, which were rapidly increasing in the country ($17.03 million). In December 2009, the MCC Board approved a further restructuring of the compact, utilizing remaining funding from the terminated rail component of the compact to target $47.2 million at energy and environmental projects and $79.7 million at rehabilitating a road and bridge.

Morocco

The five-year, $697.5 million compact, completed in September 2013, had multiple components, all aimed at increasing private sector growth. These included efforts to increase fruit tree productivity ($300.9 million), modernize the small-scale fisheries industry ($116.2 million), and support artisan crafts ($111.9 million). In addition, the compact funded financial services to micro-enterprises ($46.2 million) and provided business training and technical assistance aimed at young, unemployed graduates ($33.9 million).

Morocco has been selected as eligible for a second compact.

Mozambique

Completed in September 2013, the five-year, $506.9 million compact, like most other compacts, targeted specific districts, in this case the less prosperous north of the country. The compact had four components. Water and sanitation services were improved ($203.6 million); a major road rehabilitated ($176.3 million); land tenure services made more efficient ($39.1 million); and steps taken to protect existing coconut trees, improve coconut productivity, and support diversification to other cash crops ($17.4 million). The long-term objective was to reduce the projected poverty rate by more than 7%.

Namibia

The five-year, $304.5 million compact focuses on education, tourism, and agriculture. The education project ($145 million) will improve school infrastructure and training, vocational and skills training, and textbook acquisition. The tourism project ($67 million) will target management and infrastructure in Etosha National Park, the premier wildlife park in Namibia, and build ecotourism capacity in the country. The agriculture project ($47 million) will focus on land management, livestock support, and production of indigenous natural products.

Nicaragua

The five-year, $175 million compact with Nicaragua, ended in May 2011, focused on promoting economic growth primarily in the northwestern region of the country, where potential opportunities exist due to the area's fertile land and nearby markets in Honduras and El Salvador. The compact had three components: (1) to strengthen property registration ($26.5 million); (2) to upgrade primary and secondary roads between Managua and Leon and to provide technical assistance to the Ministry of Transportation ($92.8 million); and (3) to promote higher-profit agriculture activities, especially for poor farmers, and to improve water supply in support of higher-value sustainable agriculture.

On June 10, 2009, the MCC Board voted to terminate assistance for activities not yet contracted under the Nicaragua compact. These activities had been suspended since the end of 2008 because of the actions of the Nicaraguan government inconsistent with the MCC eligibility criteria, specifically in the area of good governance. Nicaragua first received a warning, then projects were put on hold, and then activities not yet contracted were suspended in December 2008 as the credibility of Nicaragua's municipal elections was seriously questioned. In June 2009, due to government actions that "limited the activity of political opposition, civil society, media elections and observers" prior to the municipal elections,[55] and were judged by MCC to be a pattern of action "inconsistent with the criteria used by MCC to determine eligibility for assistance,"[56] compact funding was partially terminated. The termination affected activities not yet contracted, a property regularization project and a major road, together amounting to about $62 million.

Philippines

The five-year, $434 million compact has three components. Computerization of the revenue collection process is expected to raise tax revenues and reduce tax evasion, while improving the impartiality of tax administration ($54.4 million). Support for small-scale, community development projects, designed and implemented by rural communities, is intended to strengthen local governance and participation in development activities ($120 million). Rehabilitation of 222 kilometers of road linking two provinces is meant to reduce transport costs and increase incomes ($214.4 million).

Senegal

The five-year, $540 million compact targets two infrastructure needs—roads and irrigation, both largely intended to support the agricultural sector in Senegal. The road rehabilitation project ($324 million) seeks to improve two key roads, one connecting major towns and neighboring countries to the capital and the other connecting the agricultural area of the Casamance to the rest of Senegal. The irrigation project ($170 million) will develop up to 10,500 hectares of land and prevent abandonment of 26,000 hectares. It will also address land tenure issues.

Tanzania

The five-year, $698 million compact, completed in September 2013, focused on three key economic infrastructure issues. A transport sector project ($373 million) improved major trunk roads, select rural roads, and general road maintenance capabilities, and upgraded an airport. An energy sector project ($206 million) laid an electric transmission cable from the mainland to Zanzibar and rehabilitated the existing distribution system to unserved areas. A water sector project ($66 million) expanded a clean water treatment facility serving the capital, reduced water loss in the capital region, and improved the water supply in Morogoro, a growing city.

Tanzania has been selected as eligible for a second compact.

Vanuatu

The $65.7 million, five-year compact, completed in April 2011, targeted improvements broadly in multiple types of infrastructure, including roads, wharfs, an airstrip, and warehouses. The objective was to increase the average per capita income by 15%, by helping rural agricultural producers and providers of tourism-related goods and services. The compact further aimed to help

---

[55] MCC Press Release, "MCC Urges Nicaraguan Government to Respect Democracy," available at http://www.mcc.gov/mcc/countries/nicaragua/ni-documents/release-112508-nicaragua.shtml.

[56] From Nicaragua country page of MCC website, available at http://www.mcc.gov/mcc/countries/nicaragua/index.shtml.

strengthen Vanuatu's Public Works Department in order to enhance capacity to maintain the country's entire transport network.

Zambia

The $354.8 million, five-year compact focuses entirely on the water and sanitation sector in the Lusaka area. Most of the funds ($284 million) will be used to rehabilitate and improve infrastructure; other funds will go for strengthening management and policy controlling the water sector.

Appendix C. MCC Candidate Countries FY2014

(Divided into World Bank Income Categories, as Defined by MCC Authorization)

Africa – Low Income		East Asia/Pacific – Low Income	Latin America – Low Income
Benin (FC): Second Compact Eligible FY12&13; Not FY14.	Sierra Leone: Compact eligible FY13; Not FY14	Cambodia	Haiti
Burkina Faso (C)	Somalia	Laos	
Burundi	South Sudan	Papua New Guinea	
Chad	Tanzania (FC): 2nd Compact Eligible FY13&14	Solomon Islands	**Latin America – Lower-Middle Income**
Comoros	Togo	Vietnam	
Cote D'Ivoire	Uganda	**East Asia/Pacific – Lower-Middle Income**	Bolivia *
Democratic Republic of Congo	Zambia (C)	Indonesia (C) *	El Salvador(CII)
Djibouti	**Africa – Lower Middle Income**	Kiribati *	Guatemala *: Threshold eligible FY13&14
Ethiopia	Cape Verde (CII)	Marshall Islands	Guyana
Ghana (FC): Compact Eligible FY11& 12&13&14		Micronesia *	Honduras (FC) & (TC) *
Guinea		Mongolia (FC) *	Paraguay
Kenya	**South Asia – Lower Income**	Philippines (C) *	
Lesotho (FC): Second Compact Eligible FY14	Afghanistan	Samoa	**Europe - Low Income**
Liberia (TC): Compact eligible FY13&14	Bangladesh	Timor-Leste (TC) *	None
Malawi (C)	India	Vanuatu (FC) *	**Europe – Lower-Middle Income**
Mauritania	Kyrgyz Rep.		
Mozambique (FC)	Nepal: Threshold eligible FY12&13&14		Armenia **(FC)**
Niger: Compact eligible FY13&14	Pakistan	**Mid-East – Low Income**	Georgia (CII) *
Nigeria	Tajikistan	Yemen	Kosovo
Rwanda	Uzbekistan	**Mid-East – Lower-Middle Income**	Moldova (C) *
Sao Tome & Principe	**South Asia – Lower-Middle Income**	Egypt *	Ukraine
Senegal (C)	Bhutan *	Morocco (FC): 2nd Compact Eligible FY13&14	
	Sri Lanka *		

Notes: Under MCC Authorization Rules (§606 of P.L. 108-199), Low Income = GNI per capita below World Bank International Development Association (IDA) eligibility level of $1,965 and below; Lower-Middle Income = GNI per capita income above $1,965 and below $4,085, the World Bank threshold for upper-middle income countries. Excluded from this table are countries prohibited from receiving U.S. economic assistance.

(C) = Current Compact Country; (CII) = Second Compact Country; (FC) = Former Compact Country; (TC) = Current Threshold Country.

* Countries denoted by asterisk are considered Low Income for MCC funding purposes only under P.L. 112-74, defined as bottom 75 countries in income level.

Appendix D. MCC Performance Indicators FY2013

Ruling Justly	Investing in People	Economic Freedom
Control of Corruption Source: World Bank/Brookings World Governance Indicators (WGI)	**Primary Education Expenditure as % of GDP** Sources: UNESCO and National governments	**Inflation** Source: IMF World Economic Outlook
Freedom of Information Source: Freedom House/ONI/FRINGE	**Girls' Primary Education Completion Rate (For Lower Income Countries)** Source: UNESCO or **Girls' Secondary Education Enrollment Rate (For Lower-Middle Income Countries)** Source: UNESCO	**Fiscal Policy** Source: IMF World Economic Outlook
Government Effectiveness Source: World Bank/Brookings WGI	**Health Expenditure as % of GDP** Source: World Health Organization (WHO)	**Trade Policy** Source: The Heritage Foundation
Rule of Law Source: World Bank/Brookings WGI	**Immunization Rates: DPT and Measles** Source: World Health Organization (WHO)	**Regulatory Quality** Source: World Bank/Brookings WGI
Civil Liberties Source: Freedom House	**Child Health** Sources: Columbia Center for Int'l Earth Science Info Network (CIESIN) and Yale Center for Env. Law and Policy (YCLEP)	**Business Start-Up: Days and Cost of Starting a Business** Source: International Finance Corporation
Political Rights Source: Freedom House	**Natural Resource Protection** Sources: Columbia Center for Int'l Earth Science Info Network (CIESIN) and Yale Center for Env. Law and Policy (YCLEP)	**Land Rights and Access** Source: Int'l Fund for Agricultural Development (IFAD) and Int'l Finance Corporation
		Access to Credit Source: International Finance Corporation
		Gender in the Economy Source: World Bank

Author Contact Information

Curt Tarnoff
Specialist in Foreign Affairs
ctarnoff@crs.loc.gov, 7-7656